P9-DGN-918

DISCARD

creatures of the sea

The Octopus

Other titles in the series:

Humpback Whales

Moray Eels

Rays

Sea Stars

creatures of the sea

The Octopus

Kris Hirschmann

KIDHAVEN PRESS™

THOMSON

GALE™

San Diego • Detroit • New York • San Francisco • Cleveland
New Haven, Conn. • Waterville, Maine • London • Munich

Cover photo: © Stephen Frink/CORBIS
© Fred Bavendam/Minden Pictures, 12, 22, 24, 25, 30, 31, 33, 34
© Bettmann/CORBIS, 7
© Jonathan Blair/CORBIS, 41
© Mauro Fermariello/Science Photo Library/Photo Researchers, 39
© Flip Nicklin/Minden Pictures, 28
Brandy Noon, 13
© Jeffrey L. Rotman/CORBIS, 15, 19, 21, 42
© Stuart Westmorland/CORBIS, 10, 16, 37

For more information, contact
KidHaven Press
27500 Drake Rd.
Farmington Hills, MI 48331-3535
Or you can visit our Internet site at http://www.gale.com

LIBRARY OF CONGRESS CATALOGING-IN-PUBLICATION DATA

Hirschmann, Kris, 1967–
  The octopus / by Kris Hirschmann.
    p. cm.—(Creatures of the sea)
  Includes bibliographical references (p.   ).
  Summary: Describes the physical characteristics, behavior, and life cycle of the octopus.
    ISBN 0-7377-0986-3 (hardback : alk. paper)
  1. Octopus—Juvenile literature. [1. Octopus.] I. Title. II. Series.
    QL430 .3 .02 .H585 2003
    594' .56—dc21

2001006720

Printed in the United States of America

Table of Contents

Introduction
Understanding the Octopus   6

Chapter 1
Octopus Bodies and Basics   9

Chapter 2
Eating . . . and Being Eaten   18

Chapter 3
The Octopus Life Cycle   27

Chapter 4
The Intelligent Invertebrate   36

Glossary   43

For Further Exploration   45

Index   47

Understanding the Octopus

Fishermen have been pulling octopuses out of the seas for thousands of years. The octopuses caught by ancient people were usually small. Prepared correctly, they were also tasty. Octopus flesh was (and still is) a popular food in many parts of the world, so fishermen were eager to catch and sell these creatures.

But there was also a darker side to the octopus. Long ago seamen claimed to have seen enormous octopuses on their travels. Writers made up tales of huge man-eating octopuses, and artists painted pictures of people being strangled in the octopus's grip. Because of these stories, many people feared this little-known creature. Some people even called octopuses "devilfish" to describe their supposedly evil nature.

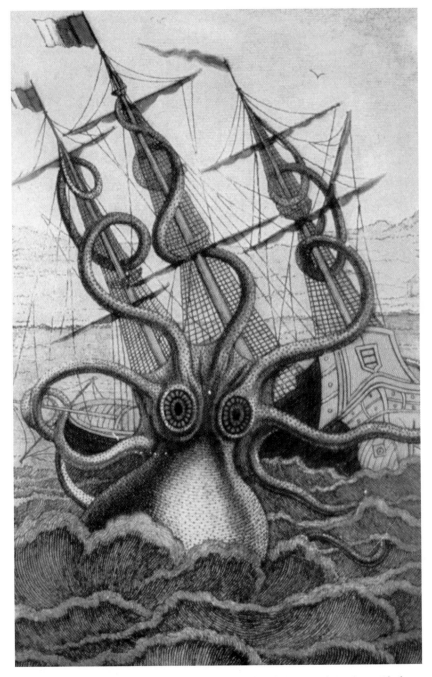

A giant octopus attacks a Spanish ship in this fanciful print from the nineteenth century.

This idea started to change, however, after underwater breathing equipment was invented in the 1950s. For the first time in history, scientists could study octopuses and other ocean creatures in their home environment. It soon became clear that octopuses were not dangerous or aggressive toward people. In fact, the opposite was true. Even the largest octopuses were gentle, curious creatures that could be approached without fear. Thanks to years of study by many scientists, octopuses no longer are seen as monsters. Instead, they are known to be shy animals with many fascinating habits and characteristics.

Greater Exposure

Public exposure has also helped improve the octopus's reputation. Aquariums around the world keep octopuses and educate people about these creatures' bodies and behaviors. Television specials show amazing scenes of octopuses in their underwater homes. Nature and diving magazines often contain articles that discuss the octopus's life and lifestyle. All of these information sources help people understand and enjoy octopuses instead of being afraid of them.

There is still a lot to learn about octopuses in the wild. No one is sure, for instance, how many octopuses exist in the world. This makes it hard to judge whether any octopus species, or types, are endangered. For now, it seems that octopus populations are holding steady. This is good news for scientists, who hope to study these fascinating creatures for many years to come.

Octopus Bodies and Basics

Octopuses are mollusks, a group of sea creatures that also includes snails, clams, slugs, and many other soft-bodied animals. Within the mollusk group, octopuses belong to a smaller group called the **cephalopods**. The word cephalopod comes from two Greek words meaning "head" and "foot." It describes animals whose "feet" grow straight out of their heads. This group includes squid, cuttlefish, and nautiluses as well as octopuses.

There are close to eight hundred different **species** of cephalopods. Of these species, more than two hundred are octopuses.

Octopuses are common around the globe. They live in every ocean in the world, including the freezing

The eight long, flowing arms of an octopus grow right out of its head.

Arctic Ocean. Not many octopuses live in chilly areas, however. Most octopuses prefer the warm tropical or subtropical waters of regions nearest the equator.

The majority of octopuses live on the ocean floor. Called bottom dwellers, these octopuses usually can be found in shallow coastal waters, making their homes in coral reefs, rocky crevices, or grassy flats near shore. But some live in the deep dark depths of the sea. Octopuses have been found crawling along the ocean floor more than three miles below the water's surface.

Some types of octopuses live in the open sea, swimming throughout their lifetimes. Water-dwelling octopuses can be found at all depths of the ocean, from the sunny surface waters to the lightless deep.

The Octopus Body

Octopuses come in a wide range of sizes. Some dwarf octopuses are tiny, measuring only about one inch from arm tip to arm tip and weighing only a few hundredths of an ounce. On the other hand, the North Pacific giant, the world's largest octopus, may be more than twenty feet across and may weigh over three hundred pounds. All other octopuses measure somewhere between these extremes. The common octopus, which is a widespread species, usually measures two to three feet across and weighs between five and ten pounds.

Octopuses are **invertebrates**. This means they have no backbone. In fact, they have no bones at all. Most invertebrates have hard shells that protect their soft bodies, but octopuses do not. They are soft all over except for a tough mouth. Some octopuses also have small hard bits buried deep inside their heads. These hard bits are evidence that octopus ancestors had shells. Over many millions of years, the shells got smaller and smaller and eventually disappeared inside the octopuses' bodies.

Because it has no supporting bones or shell, an octopus looks very strange if it is taken out of the water. Gravity pulls the animal's body into a shapeless, slimy blob. In its home environment, however, the octopus gets all the support it needs from the surrounding water. Its body spreads out and takes on the typical octopus shape: a rounded head attached to eight long, flexible arms.

A North Pacific giant octopus easily squeezes itself through this four-inch hole.

An octopus can do some incredible things with its soft body. It can arrange itself into different shapes to suit the situation. It also can pass through very small cracks and holes. Scientists once saw a foot-long octopus with a head the size of a tennis ball squeeze itself through a half-inch hole. This ability is very helpful to a hunting octopus that may need to chase its prey into tight areas. An octopus can also force its flexible body into small spaces when it needs to hide from enemies.

An Amazing Head

The octopus's brain, stomach, heart, and other internal organs are located inside its head. In fact, the head is really nothing but a soft bag of organs held together by the octopus's skin, which is called the **mantle**. The mouth is found on the bottom of the head, right where the octopus's arms meet.

The head also contains the octopus's eyes. Octopuses have excellent vision. Although they cannot see colors, octopuses can judge the size, shape, and brightness of objects. They also can poke up the part of their head that contains their eyes. This little lift is just enough to help the octopus get a better look around.

Octopuses breathe by sucking water across their gills, which are found inside the head in an area called the mantle cavity. The gills take oxygen from the water. Then the octopus squeezes the water out through

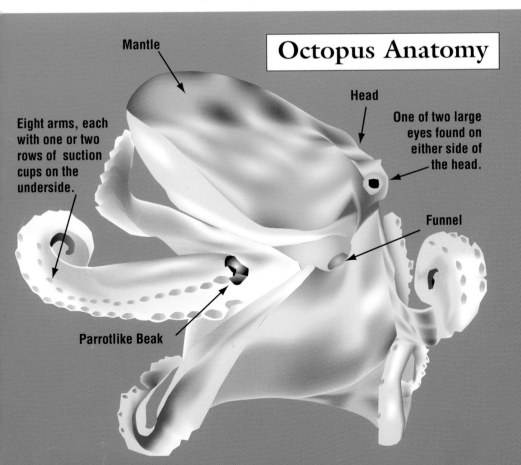

Mantle

Octopus Anatomy

Head

One of two large eyes found on either side of the head.

Eight arms, each with one or two rows of suction cups on the underside.

Funnel

Parrotlike Beak

a flexible tube, called a **funnel**, or siphon, that is located close to the octopus's eyes, near the bottom of the head.

An octopus can use its funnel as a kind of "jet engine" when it needs to make a speedy getaway. The octopus sucks water into its head, then squeezes hard to force the water out through the funnel at a high speed. The sudden blast pushes the octopus very quickly through the water and helps it escape from danger.

Arms and Suckers

Eight rubbery arms are attached to the octopus's head. Like every other part of the octopus, the arms have no bones and are very flexible. The octopus can twist, curl, and bend its arms into hundreds of different positions.

Each of the octopus's eight arms is lined with round disks called **suckers**. Some species have just one row of suckers on each arm. Other species have two rows. The suckers vary in size depending on their position. Those near the octopus's head are the largest, while the ones near the arm tips may be tiny.

The main purpose of the suckers is to grab and hold things. The octopus places its suckers against an object, then uses its muscles to pull up on the centers of the suckers. This action creates suction that makes the object cling to the suckers. By relaxing its muscles, the octopus releases the pressure and lets go of the object.

The octopus also uses its suckers to taste and feel things. Tiny receptors on the edges of each sucker pick up taste and touch messages and send them to the octopus's brain. Using its suckers, an octopus can tell whether an animal is good to eat just by touching it.

The octopus's arms are used for more than just holding and hunting. They also may be used for walking. Bottom-dwelling octopuses often creep from place to place along the ocean floor, pulling themselves along with their incredible arms.

Masters of Disguise

Despite its unusual shape, an octopus can be hard to spot in its ocean home. This is because octopuses are masters of disguise. They have the ability to change their skin texture and color at will. An octopus can blend so well into its surroundings that it becomes almost impossible to see it.

An octopus uses its suckers to hold onto its next meal, a dead cabezon fish.

Octopuses change their color by expanding or contracting tiny organs in their skin. These organs are called **chromatophores**, and they can be yellow, orange, red, brown, or black. An octopus's skin also contains reflecting cells that can bounce back surrounding colors like bright blue, green, and other colors not found in the chromatophores. By making some chromatophores and reflecting cells big and others small, the octopus can instantly transform its skin color and pattern.

An octopus can change its skin texture too. Using many tiny muscles, the octopus pushes its skin up

By changing the texture of its skin, an octopus blends into its surroundings.

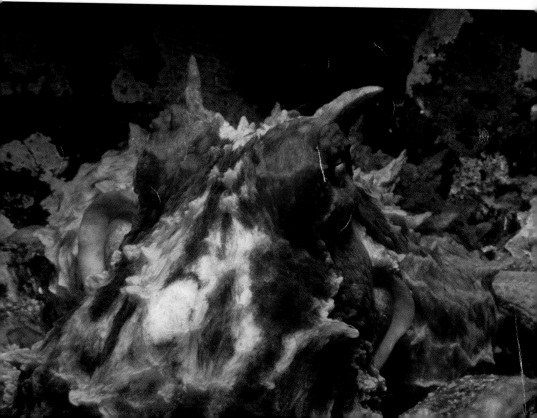

into thousands of small bumps. This rough texture helps the octopus hide or **camouflage** itself against rocks, coral, and other uneven surfaces.

Some colors and textures also seem to show how an octopus is feeling. When an octopus is angry, it may turn red or another dark color and develop bumps on its skin. It may turn white and smooth when it is frightened. An octopus even may "blink" skin patterns on and off. Scientists believe that these and other color signals help octopuses communicate with each other.

Whatever an octopus's color or texture, one thing is certain. Octopuses are the camouflage champions of the natural world. This ability is just one of the skills that makes the octopus such an amazing and interesting animal.

Eating . . . and Being Eaten

Octopuses are carnivores, which means they eat the flesh of other animals. Octopuses mostly eat lobsters, crabs, and shelled mollusks such as clams, scallops, and oysters. They eat fish if they can catch them. They even will eat other octopuses from time to time.

An octopus does not have any trouble finding and eating its prey. It has many tools and tricks that make it a skillful hunter.

Catching Prey

Octopuses have many ways of catching prey. The easiest technique is called the ambush. In ambush hunting, an octopus hides or camouflages itself and waits for prey to approach. Sometimes an octopus even might wiggle one arm tip as a lure. When an unsus-pecting crab, fish, or other prey animal gets close enough, the octopus either pounces or reaches out and grabs the prey with several powerful arms.

An octopus also may hunt by crawling around on the ocean floor, poking its arms into rocky cracks and crevices. If the octopus finds a hidden animal, it seizes it with an arm and attaches its powerful suckers. When the octopus pulls its arm out of the crack, a meal comes with it.

The most unusual hunting technique that octo-puses use is called **parachuting**. In this method, an octopus swims slowly above the ocean floor, looking for prey. When the octopus spots a tasty animal below,

An octopus gracefully spreads its arms as it prepares to close in on unsuspecting prey.

it turns upright and spreads its eight arms wide. Using the skin between its arms as a parachute to control its descent, the octopus glides down silently. It lands on top of the prey and quickly closes its **web**, trapping the startled animal inside.

Dangerous Mouths

Once the octopus has caught its prey, it must kill it. It may do this by biting hard with its mouth, which is sharp and pointed. (Because of its shape, an octopus's hard mouth is usually called a **beak**.) Soft-bodied prey like fish are easy to kill by biting alone. The octopus also may inject venom from two glands near its beak. The venom paralyzes and eventually kills the prey.

An octopus may not have to inject the venom to kill its prey. Scientists believe that octopuses sometimes surround animals with their web, then simply release their venom into the water inside the web. Without any way to reach fresh water, the trapped prey must breathe the octopus's poison. The prey weakens quickly and soon stops struggling.

All octopuses are poisonous to their prey. But most are not harmful to humans. A bite that would be deadly to a crab or a lobster might feel no worse than a bee sting to a person. And the bites of many octopus species have no effect at all on people.

There is one exception to this rule. The blue-ringed octopus of Australia is deadly to humans. In fact, it is one of the most dangerous animals in the

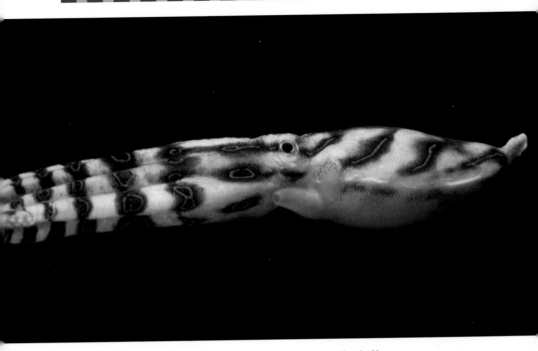

The tiny blue-ringed octopus can easily kill a person with a single bite.

world. Although the blue-ringed octopus measures just four inches from arm tip to arm tip, it is so poisonous that its bite can usually kill an adult human within five minutes.

Time to Eat

An octopus cannot swallow large chunks of food. First the octopus must use its sharp beak to tear the flesh of its prey into small pieces. Soft prey are eaten quickly using this method. Crabs, shrimp, and lobsters are a bit more challenging, but the octopus can usually tear their limbs off without much trouble. Removing the limbs leaves holes in their shells through which the octopus can attack the prey's flesh.

Clams and other shelled mollusks are harder to eat. Their tough shells protect them from the octopus's bite. This armor, however, does not stop the octopus for long. The octopus simply holds the prey tight and starts rubbing its rough tongue against the shell. This tongue, which is called the **radula**, can drill a hole through the thickest shell. While it drills, the octopus also releases chemicals that soften the shell a little bit. This makes the drilling job easier.

A North Pacific giant octopus uses its tongue to drill through the shells of two crabs before eating the meat.

After the octopus has made a hole, it injects chemicals that paralyze the prey. These chemicals also start to dissolve the prey's muscles. Soon the prey becomes so weak that it cannot hold its shell closed. The animal flops open, and the octopus grabs its meal.

The radula does more than just drill through shells. The octopus also can use its rough tongue to scrape all the meat from the insides of crabs' and lobsters' shells. The radula works like sandpaper, pulling every last bit of food away from the shell and into the hungry octopus's mouth.

Efficient Eaters

Depending on its lifestyle, an octopus can eat 2 to 4 percent of its body weight each day. Warmth speeds up body processes, so warm-water octopuses need more food than their cold-water relatives. And active octopuses need to eat more often than those that spend a lot of time resting.

Octopuses hunt as long as is necessary to catch the food they need. On a good day, an octopus might fill its stomach in an hour or two. On a bad day, it might need to hunt continually to satisfy its hunger. Octopuses that eat mostly clams and other small mollusks tend to hunt often because their meals take so long to eat.

All octopuses have one thing in common. Their bodies are very good at converting food into octopus flesh. About half of the food eaten by an octopus may

An octopus gobbles up a fish. Octopuses rapidly increase their body size after eating.

become body weight. Under perfect eating conditions, an octopus can double its size in a week.

Octopus Defenses

Although octopuses are skilled hunters, they are not the only predators out looking for food. Moray eels, sharks, and other hungry animals roam the same areas where octopuses are found. If an octopus runs into one of these creatures, it may wind up as a meal.

Octopuses have many defenses to prevent this from happening. Their best defense is to avoid being noticed at all. An octopus uses its color- and texture-changing abilities to achieve this goal. It also can hide by squeezing its soft body into tiny cracks and holes.

If a predator does catch sight of an octopus, the octopus may use a defense called **inking**. Inside the

An octopus squirts ink to defend itself as it jets away from a predator.

octopus's head is a sac filled with dark brown or black liquid. When an octopus is threatened, it can blast a cloud of this liquid out of its funnel. The ink blocks the predator's sight and may also affect its sense of smell. While the predator is confused, the octopus changes color and jets off to safety.

Shedding Arms

Sometimes hiding and inking fail, and a predator manages to grab one of the octopus's arms. If this happens, the octopus can escape by shedding its arm. Doing this does not hurt the octopus, and the arm grows back after a few months.

Unfortunately for the octopus, none of its defenses do much good against human fishermen. People take hundreds of thousands of pounds of octopuses out of the seas each year. But so far, human fishing activities do not seem to be harming octopus populations. There are still plenty of octopuses living

The Octopus Life Cycle

Octopuses are not long-lived animals. The largest octopuses may live three to four years, but most do not live nearly that long. An octopus of average size lives about a year, and the lives of smaller octopuses are even shorter.

The octopus's short life span makes it easy to study this creature at all stages of its life. Scientists have learned that an octopus's life follows a predictable—but fascinating—cycle.

The Infant Phase

Octopuses hatch from eggs. As soon as they hatch, they are swept away by the ocean currents. Infant octopuses must make their own way in the world without any help from a mother or father.

A transparent baby octopus is swept away from its mother and will have to live on its own.

Most newly hatched octopuses are about an eighth of an inch long—half the length of a pencil eraser. The baby octopuses' heads account for most of this length. At this stage, the eight arms are just little stumps. These tiny creatures drift through the ocean waters, going wherever the current takes them.

Although newly hatched octopuses are tiny, they are already skilled hunters. They catch and feed on protozoa (single-celled animals) and other small prey that float near the water's surface. A baby octopus grows quickly, doubling in size every week or two. Its arms get longer and its muscles get stronger.

Some octopuses spend their entire lives floating with the ocean currents. But most octopuses are bottom dwellers. When they get big enough, babies of bottom-dwelling species migrate to the ocean floor. Most octopuses are ready to make this important move within one to two months after hatching. Once they reach the sea floor, the little octopuses are ready to start their adult lives.

Finding a Home

The octopus's first task is to find a home. An octopus's home is called a den or a **lair**. Octopuses are most comfortable in tight spaces and often choose to make their dens in coral reefs or rock piles. They also set up housekeeping in pots, cans, jars, and other trash.

If an octopus cannot find a home it likes, it may build one itself. Octopuses are known to arrange rocks, shells, and other hard materials into little caves. This habit can be very annoying to people who keep octopuses as pets. One small octopus can rearrange an entire aquarium overnight.

An octopus leaves its den to hunt, but it often brings its catch home to eat. When the octopus is done with its meal, it tosses the empty shells of its prey out the front door of its home. Over time, the octopus may build a good-sized pile of debris. Scuba divers and scientists look for these piles when they are trying to find octopuses. It is much easier to spot an octopus's garbage than it is to find the octopus itself.

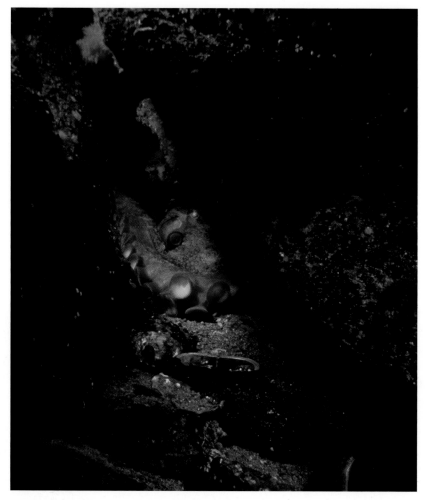

The entrance to this octopus's den is littered with abalone shells from its previous meals.

Octopuses are solitary animals. They live and hunt alone. So only one octopus occupies any den.

Mating

After four to eight months, most octopuses are fully grown adults. They are now ready to find a mate and create baby octopuses of their own.

The mating process begins when a male and a female octopus find each other. The male has a special arm called a **hectocotylus**. He puts this arm under the female's mantle and passes several spermatophores into her body. The spermatophores are the seeds that will fertilize the female's eggs.

The mating process may take as little as a minute, or it may take several hours. When it is done, the octopuses go their separate ways. The female carries the male's spermatophores with her.

A small, red male octopus mates with a large, gray female on the ocean floor.

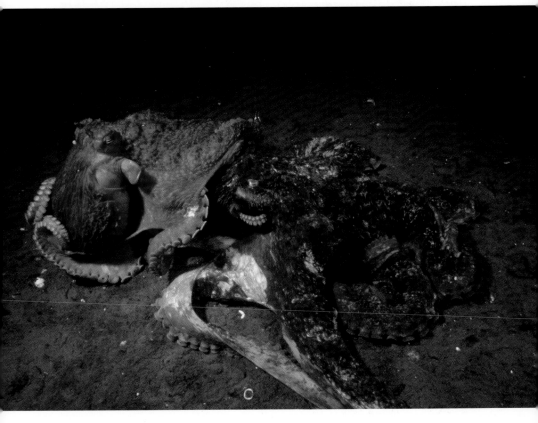

A female octopus may not use the spermatophores right away. It could be several weeks before the female's body is ready to create eggs. Until that time, the female will store the spermatophores inside her body.

Laying the Eggs

When the female is ready, she starts to develop her eggs. The number of eggs depends on the species. Some octopus species lay just a few large eggs. Others lay more than one hundred thousand tiny eggs.

A few types of octopuses carry their eggs with them wherever they go. Most octopuses, however, find a comfortable hole and set up a nursery lair. An octopus will lay her eggs in this lair, then stay and protect them until they hatch.

In order to keep her eggs from being swept away, the mother octopus uses a sticky substance to glue them down. She glues each egg individually, so the egg-laying process may take weeks. Some octopuses glue their eggs directly to the walls and ceiling of the lair. Others attach the eggs in hanging clusters that contain more than a thousand eggs each. Each egg in these clusters looks like a grain of white rice hanging from a slender thread.

Guarding the Eggs

After the octopus has laid her eggs, she uses her body to block the lair's entrance. Until the eggs hatch, the octopus stands guard against fish, eels, crabs, and other predators.

Besides protecting the eggs, the octopus has another important job. She must keep her eggs clean. The octopus does this by squirting the eggs with water from her funnel. She also may use her littlest suckers to gently stroke dirt, fungi, and parasites off the eggs.

Taking care of the eggs is a twenty-four-hour-a-day job. The octopus cannot leave the lair for even a moment without putting her eggs at risk. So the female keeps her guard around the clock. She does not hunt. In fact, she does not eat at all, even if a crab or another tasty animal crawls right past the lair.

An octopus guards her eggs, seen here dangling beneath a boulder.

It takes two to five months for the eggs of most octopuses to hatch. During this time, the mother grows weaker and weaker from lack of food. Her life is coming to an end. Some female octopuses die before their eggs hatch. Others live long enough to see their babies emerge.

The Hatch

All of the baby octopuses hatch around the same time. Water currents sweep the tiny infants out of the lair, away from the mother who has guarded them so carefully.

Right away, predators attack the swarm of babies. Hungry fish and other creatures gobble down thousands of little octopuses.

Many of the babies escape the initial attack and float up to the sunny surface waters. There they start

A helpless newborn octopus drifts away from eggs that are about to hatch.

eating and growing. But the babies are still tiny, and they cannot protect themselves against larger predators. Sea birds, fish, and other animals continue to feast on the hatchlings. Within a few weeks, almost all of the babies will have died.

A very few of the infant octopuses get lucky. They avoid predators, and they become big and strong enough to migrate to the ocean floor. Only ten to twenty octopuses from the original hatch live long enough to make this journey, and even fewer will reach adulthood. But it is enough. It only takes a few young octopuses to continue the cycle of life.

The Intelligent Invertebrate

As animals go, octopuses are quite intelligent. They have been showing their smarts for centuries by stealing fish out of nets and lobsters out of traps. In recent decades, octopuses have been the subjects of many scientific studies designed to gauge their intelligence. Scientists now agree that octopuses are probably the smartest of all invertebrates.

Signs of Intelligence

Just how smart is an octopus? No one knows for sure. Some scientists think octopuses may be about as intelligent as house cats. But other scientists point out that an invertebrate's brain is not like a **vertebrate**'s brain, so intelligence may mean something very different in an octopus than it does in a bird, reptile, or mammal.

Still, there is no denying that octopuses do some smart things. For instance, some octopuses have learned to recognize divers who visit them regularly. And they remember these divers for a long time. Even if a diver visits only once in a while, the octopus will approach without fear—a sure sign that the diver looks familiar.

A friendly octopus greets a scuba diver. Octopuses are able to recognize divers who visit often.

Octopuses also may make mental maps of their home territory. An octopus often crawls for a long distance when it hunts. It takes a twisted, confusing path as it travels. But when the octopus is ready to return home, it leaves the ocean floor and swims straight back to its den. It does not have to retrace its route. According to some scientists, this behavior shows intelligence.

Octopuses in one aquarium were even seen playing. The octopuses used their funnels to squirt jets of water at an empty plastic bottle, pushing it back and forth. Until this behavior was observed, scientists thought that only vertebrates were smart enough to play. These playful octopuses were doing more than just squirting water at a bottle, though. They were showing signs of intelligent behavior.

Problem Solvers

The ability to solve problems is another sign of intelligence. Several experiments have shown that octopuses have this important ability.

In one famous experiment, scientists put a live lobster inside a see-through glass jar. Then they plugged the mouth of the jar with a cork and put it near an octopus's home. The octopus came out immediately and started trying to eat the lobster. First it grabbed at the lobster with its arms, but it was blocked by the glass of the jar. So the octopus tried another hunting technique. It wrapped the entire jar in its web, then tried to poison it. This did not work either.

But the octopus did not give up. It kept trying to get the lobster. After about three hours, the octopus finally pulled the cork out of the jar. Within seconds, the hungry octopus had grabbed the lobster and started eating it.

It is possible that the octopus pulled the cork out by accident. But the scientists who ran this experiment do not think so. They believe that the octopus figured out how to release the lobster from the jar. The octopus learned that its normal methods would not work, and it kept trying new things until it finally accomplished its task.

Training the Octopus

So it seems that an octopus can solve problems. But can it actually be trained to do things, as a dog or a cat can be trained? Scientists have done many experiments that tried to answer this question.

An octopus is tested to see if it can recognize colors in this laboratory tank.

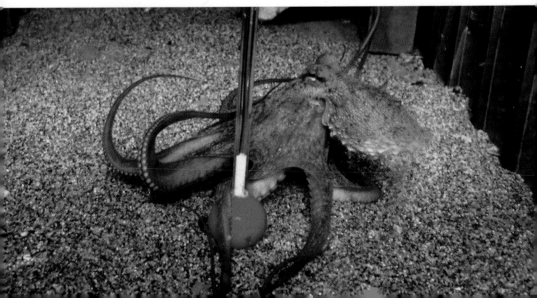

In one of these experiments, scientists hoped to train an octopus to grab a black disk but avoid a white disk. To do this, they set up a system of reward and punishment. If the octopus touched a black disk, it would get food. If it touched a white disk, it would get a small electric shock.

The scientists in charge of the experiment thought it would take the octopus a while to learn the meaning of the disks. But the octopus turned out to be even smarter than they thought. The octopus touched the white disk only once. After that, it would not go anywhere near the white disk. It went straight for the black disk every time. The octopus learned its lesson in just one try.

Other experiments have had similar results. Octopuses have been trained to poke their arms into holes in a wall to get food. Some have learned how to get through mazes. Some have even been trained to recognize simple shapes like squares and crosses. All of these experiments provide evidence that octopuses are, indeed, among the smartest animals in the sea.

Octopus vs. Human

Using their natural intelligence and their soft bodies, octopuses are escape artists. They can find the tiniest crack in an aquarium top, then squeeze themselves through it to freedom.

Once out of the tank, the octopus moves toward open water. If there is no open water, the octopus may just crawl around making trouble. In one case,

An octopus reaches out from its clay-pot home to touch the hand of a scuba diver who is removing objects from a sunken ship.

an octopus escaped from a home aquarium and crawled into a nearby study. The owner found the octopus pulling books off the shelves and flipping through their pages.

Another interesting case occurred at a large public aquarium. Employees noticed that animals were disappearing from the tanks during the night, so they put up a video camera to see what was going on. They discovered that an octopus was climbing out of its tank and into the other animals' tanks. The octopus would eat its fill, then return to its home. In the morning, the thief was always found right where it belonged.

A scientist inspects a dead octopus aboard a research ship off the coast of British Columbia, Canada.

This kind of behavior fascinates scientists. It makes them want to learn more about octopuses and their amazing intelligence. However, it is not easy to study octopus behavior. An octopus brain works very differently from a human brain, so understanding the octopus well enough to design good experiments is a challenge. The octopus's short life span is another challenge. Small- to medium-sized octopuses do not live long, so scientists may have only a few months to work with any individual animal.

Because of these and other factors, knowledge of octopus behavior and intelligence may come slowly. But it is sure to come. Octopuses are too interesting to go unstudied. Over time, much more will be learned about these fascinating creatures.

Glossary

beak: An octopus's sharp, pointed mouth.

camouflage: Skin coloring and/or patterns designed to blend into the background.

cephalopod: An animal whose arms are attached directly to its head.

chromatophores: Color cells in the skin that can expand or contract, thereby changing the octopus's color.

funnel: A flexible tube in the octopus's head. Water and ink are pushed out through the funnel.

hectocotylus: A male octopus's mating arm.

inking: The process of squirting dark liquid at an attacker.

invertebrate: Any animal that does not have a backbone.

lair: The resting or sleeping place of a wild animal.

mantle: The skin that covers the octopus's head.

parachuting: Floating downward with the arms spread wide, using the web as a parachute.

radula: The octopus's rough tongue.

species: A biological classification that describes a specific type of animal.

suckers: Round suction disks that line the octopus's arms.

vertebrate: Any animal that has a backbone.

web: Thin skin found between the upper parts of an octopus's arms.

For Further Exploration

Books and Periodicals

Fred Bavendam, "Eye to Eye with the Giant Octopus," *National Geographic*, March 1991. This fascinating article is full of great information about the giant octopuses of British Columbia. It includes lots of stunning color photos.

James Martin, *Tentacles: The Amazing World of Octopus, Squid, and Their Relatives*. New York: Crown, 1993. Learn a little bit about the entire cephalopod family in this easy-to-read book.

Noel Peattie, *Hydra and Kraken, Or, the Lore and Lure of Lake-Monsters and Sea-Serpents*. Oakland, CA: Regent Press, 1996. Read about some of the legendary sea monsters that once made people fear the octopus.

Jules Verne with Judith Conaway, *20,000 Leagues Under the Sea*. New York: Random House, 1988. This version of Verne's classic underwater tale is specially adapted for younger readers.

Websites

The Cephalopod Page (is.dal.ca). This scientific site includes lots of cephalopod information, pictures, and links.

The Octopus News Magazine Online (www.tonmo. com). This site includes all kinds of great information about octopuses. It features a weekly octopus survey, listings of upcoming TV shows that feature octopuses, and a cool area just for kids.

Index

aquariums
  behavior and, 40–41
  education and, 8
arms
  of babies, 28
  described, 14–15
  hectocotylus, 31

babies, 27–29, 34–35
beaks, 20–21
behavior, 40–41
blue-ringed octopuses, 20–21
bodies
  arms, 14–15, 28, 31
  flexibility of, 12, 40
  head, 12–14, 28
  mouth, 20–21
  radula, 22–23
  shape of, 11
  skin, 15–17, 25
bottom dwellers, 10
breathing, 13–14

camouflage
  ambush hunting and, 18
  defense and, 25
  described, 15–17
cephalopods, 9
characteristics, 8, 30
chromatophores, 15–17
clams

described, 9
  eating, 22–23
  as prey, 18
coloration, 15–17, 25
common octopus species, 11
communication, 17
crabs, 18, 21
cuttlefish, 9

defenses, 14, 25–26
dens, 29–30, 32
devilfish, 6

eating
  debris from, 29
  guarding eggs and,
    33, 34
  type of prey and, 21–23
education, 8
eggs
  care of, 32–34
  hatching from, 27, 34
  laying, 32
  mating and, 31–32
experiments, 38–40
eyes, 13

fish, 18, 35
funnels, 13–14, 38

gills, 13–14

habitat, 9–10
heads, 12–14, 28
hectocotylus, 31
homes, 29–30, 32
hunting
  by ambush, 18–19
  by babies, 28
  by crawling, 15, 19
  flexible bodies and, 12
  killing prey, 20–21
  by parachuting, 19–21
  time spent, 23

inking, 25–26
intelligence
  signs of, 36, 37–38, 41
  studying, 38–40, 41–42
invertebrates
  brains of, 36
  shells and, 11

lairs, 29–30, 32
life spans, 27, 42
lobsters, 18, 21

mantle, 13
mating, 30–32
mollusks
  described, 9
  eating, 22–23
  types of prey, 18
moray eels, 25
motion, 15, 19
mouths, 20–21

nautiluses, 9

oysters, 18

parachuting, 19–21
playing, 38
poison, 20, 21, 23
prey
  of babies, 28
  eggs as, 32–33
  killing, 20–21
  octopuses as, 25–26
  types of, 18
problem solving, 38–39
protozoa, 28

radula, 22–23

scallops, 18
sea birds, 35
sharks, 25
shrimp, 21
sight, sense of, 13
sizes, 11
skin, 15–17, 25
slugs, 9
snails, 9
species, 9
speed, 14
spermatophores, 31–32
squid, 9
suckers, 14–15

taste, sense of, 14–15
tongues, 22–23
touch, sense of, 14–15
training, 40

venom, 20, 21, 23
vision, 13

webs, 20